I0236200

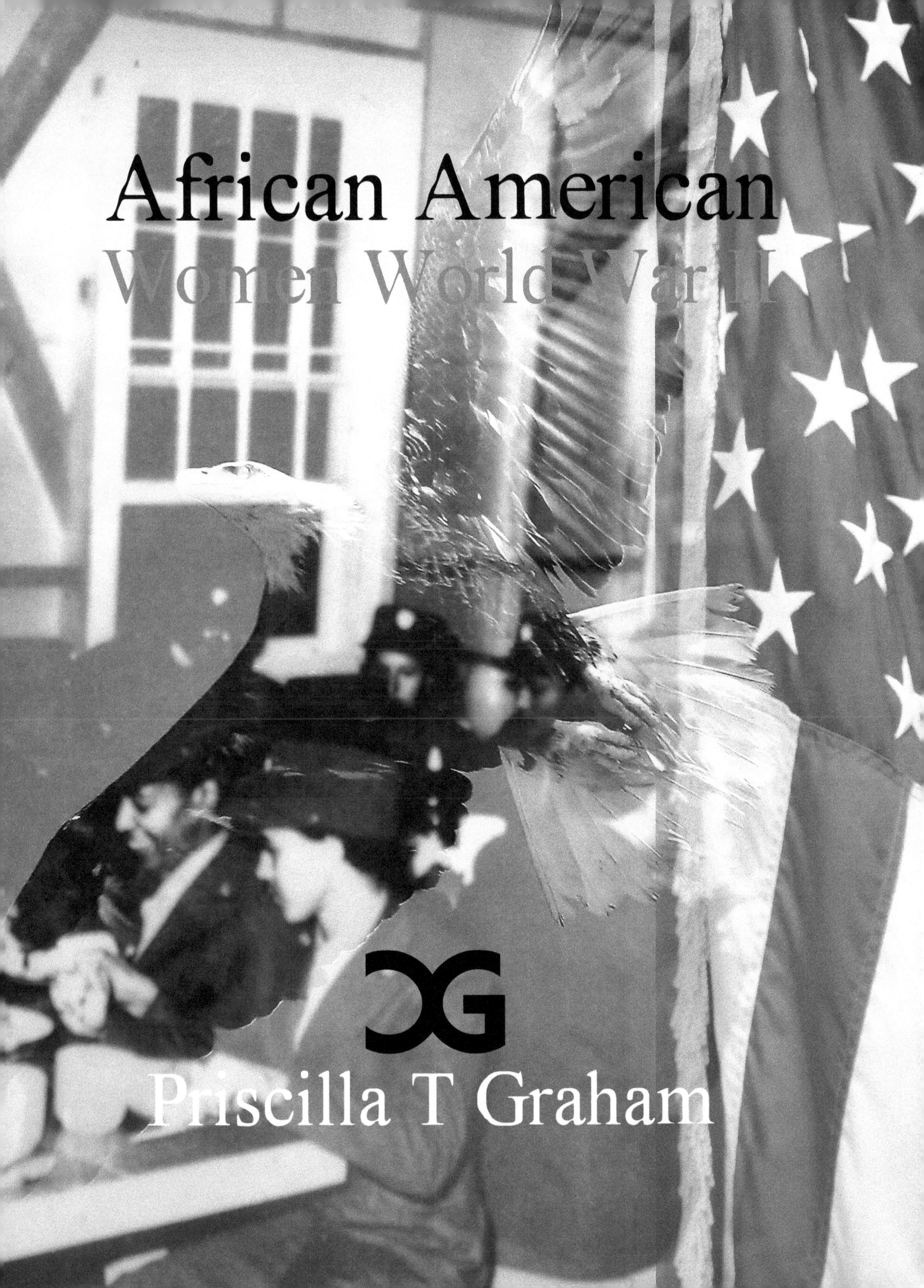

African American Women World War II

Priscilla T Graham

ISBN: 978-1-953824-06-6
African American Women World War II

Printed in the United States of America

Cover design and book layout by Priscilla T Graham

In the making of this book, every attempt has been made to verify names, facts, and figures.

Photos Public Domain

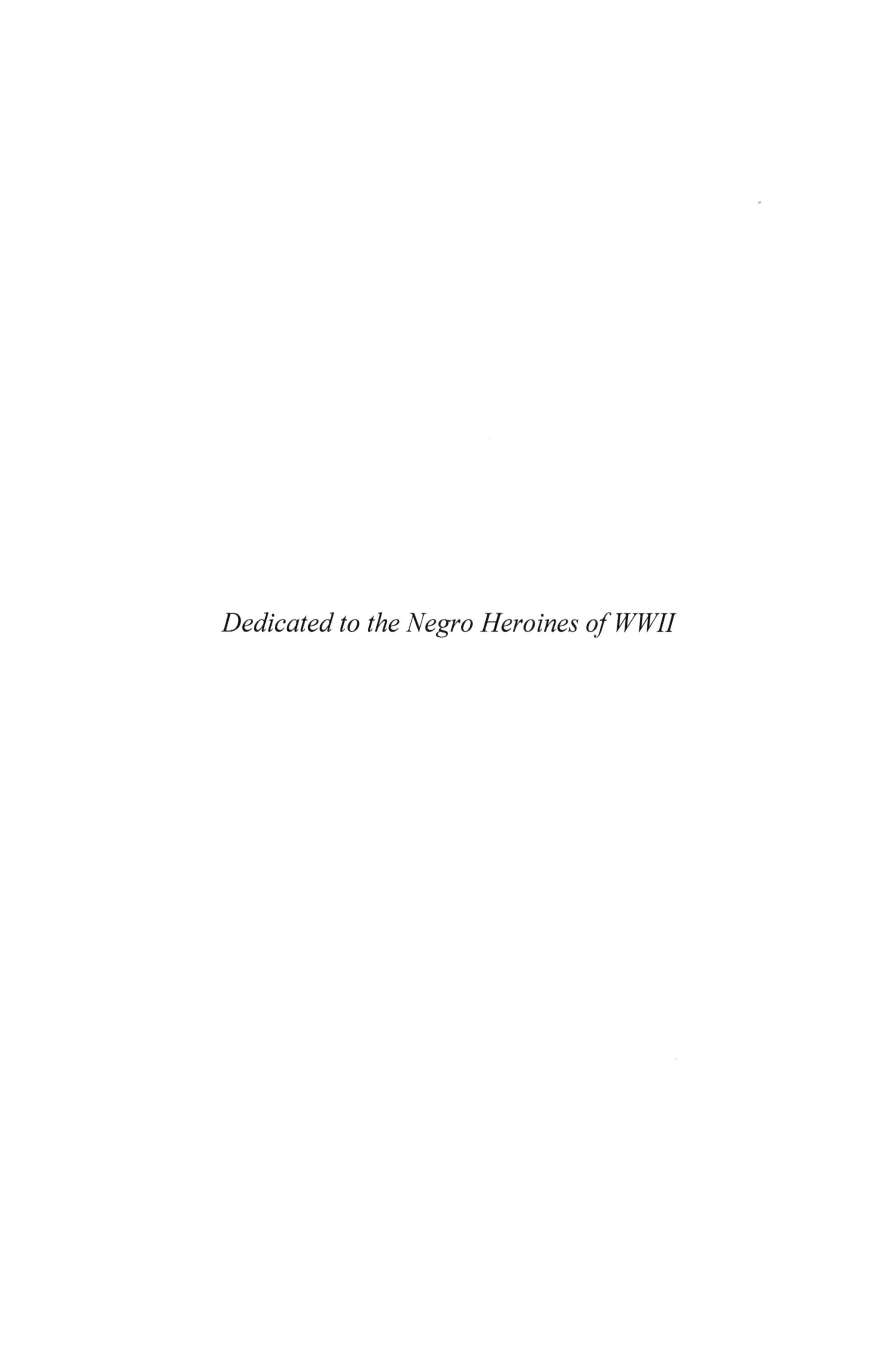

Dedicated to the Negro Heroines of WWII

Contents

Women!
Answer
America's
Call

SERVE IN THE W.A.A.C.

World War II

Over 50 countries fought on the battlegrounds of Asia, Europe, North Africa, the Atlantic and Pacific Oceans, and the Mediterranean Sea in one of the world's most deadly and costliest wars in world history, World War II. The United States entered the war in 1941 after Japanese planes bombed Pearl Harbor, Hawaii on December 7, 1941.

Research estimates that during World War II over 2.5 million Negro men registered for the draft, and large numbers of Negro women volunteered to serve in the Army, Army Air Forces, Navy, Marine Corps, and Coast Guard. Although these men and women experienced discrimination and segregation, they served their country with great distinction and made valuable contributions to the war efforts.

President Franklin D. Roosevelt signed a declaration of war against Japan on December 8, 1941, the day after Japanese forces attacked the United States Military Base at Pearl Harbor, Hawaii.

Oveta Culp Hobby being sworn in as the first Director of the Women's Army Auxiliary Corps by Major General Myron C. Cramer along with General George C. Marshall and Secretary of War Henry L. Stimson.

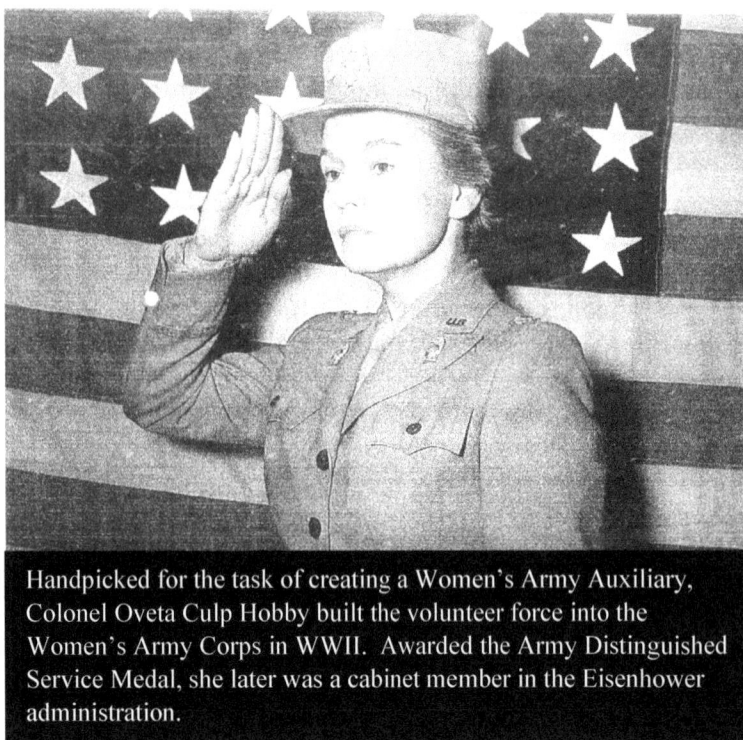

Handpicked for the task of creating a Women's Army Auxiliary, Colonel Oveta Culp Hobby built the volunteer force into the Women's Army Corps in WWII. Awarded the Army Distinguished Service Medal, she later was a cabinet member in the Eisenhower administration.

WAC History

The Honorable Edith Nourse Rogers, Congresswoman from Massachusetts, introduced the first bill to establish a Women's Auxiliary on May 28, 1941.

On May 14, 1942, Congress approved the creation of a Women's Army Auxiliary Corps, WAAC. The WAAC was established for the purpose of making available to the national defense the knowledge, skill, and special training of women of the nation. Two days later, Colonel Mrs. Oveta Culp Hobby was appointed the first Director of the WAAC.

During World War II, Mary Macleod Bethune served as a special assistant to the secretary of war and assistant to director of the Women's Army Auxiliary Corps. She organized the first women's officer candidate schools. First Lady Eleanor Roosevelt and civil rights leader Dr. Mary McLeod Bethune called for Negro women to serve as enlisted personnel and officers in the WAAC.

Five training centers were opened within a year. The first at Fort Des Moines, Iowa, the second at Daytona Beach, Florida, the third at Fort Oglethorpe, Georgia, the fourth at Fort Devens, Massachusetts, and the fifth at Camp Ruston, Louisiana. As an Auxiliary of the Army, the WAAC had no military status-they could not receive overseas pay and were ineligible for government life insurance; therefore Mrs. Rogers introduced another bill in January 1943 to enlist and commission women in the Army or Reserves of the United States. This would allow women to serve overseas and free a man to fight.

President Franklin D. Roosevelt signed the bill on July 1, 1943 and 90 days later the WAAC was discontinued and in its place, was the Women's Army Corps, WAC. This gave women the rank, privileges, and benefits as male soldiers.

Six months before women received military status, the first WAAC contingent arrived in Algeria, North Africa.

In July 1943, the first WAAC Separate Battalion arrived in England led by Lieutenant Colonel Mary A. Hallaren. Three

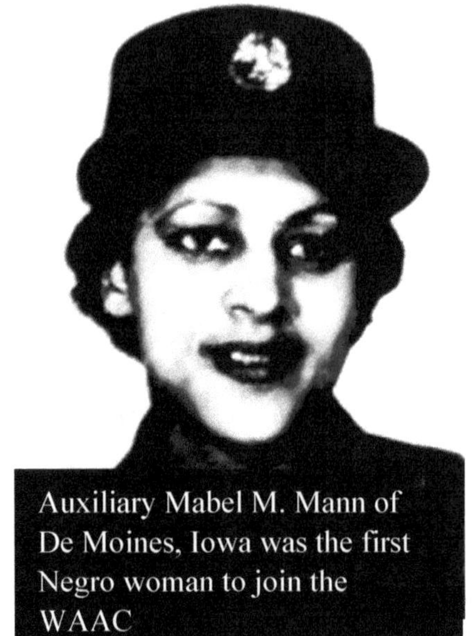

Auxiliary Mabel M. Mann of De Moines, Iowa was the first Negro woman to join the WAAC

Dr. Mary Macleod Bethune and First Lady Eleanor Roosevelt

Recruiting

Lieutenants Harriett West and Irma Cayton going over recruiting schedule report at WAAC Headquarters, Temp Building M, 26th Street in Washington, DC. 1942

WAC's joined Vice Admiral Lord Louis Mountbatten's Southeast Asia Command in New Delhi, India, October 1943.

A WAC platoon arrived in Caserta, Italy in November and a month later another arrived in Cairo, Egypt. January 1944 marked the arrival of the first WAC's in the Pacific at New Caledonia and in May a large group arrived in Sydney, Australia.

With several units of white woman sent to serve the European Theater of the War, Negro organizations pressed the War Department to extend the opportunity to serve overseas to Negro WAC.

Pallas Athene

As its symbol, the WAAC adopted Pallas Athene, Greek goddess of victory and womanly virtue - wise in peace and in the arts of war.

The traditional US and Pallas Athene were worn as lapel insignia. The cap insignia was an eagle, adapted from the design of the Army eagle. The WAAC eagle, later familiarly known as *the Buzzard*, was also imprinted on the plastic buttons of the uniform.

Group of ten women and WAAC in uniform posing with Women's Army Auxiliary Corp posters inscribed *You Can Count On Me Uncle WAACS* and Join the *WAAC Your Vocation*

Negro US Army WAAC Mary K. Adair taking an examination for Officer's Candidate School, Fort McPherson, Georgia on June 20, 1942.

Jesse Ward, Natalie Donaldson, Vera Campbell, Verneal Austin, and Glendora Moore contingents leaving the US Army building for basic training at Des Moines, Iowa, July 20, 1942

Uniform Distribution

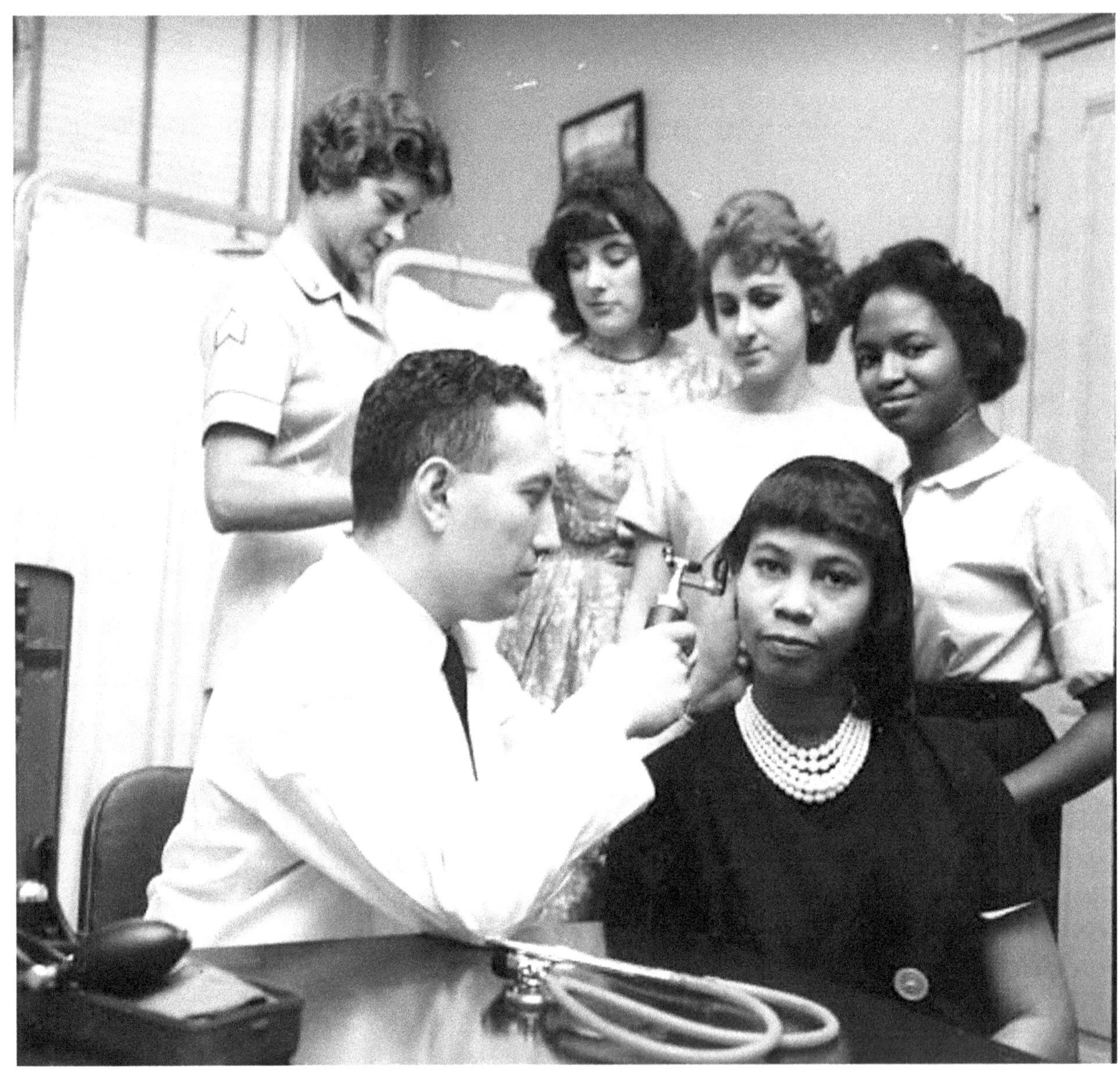

Captain Luige Mazzella, MD, Chief Medical Officer checking Wilma J. Glenn of Huntington, Long Island ears waiting their turn are Lois Hart, Brooklyn; Carmela La Sala, Bronx; Carol Comerford, Amityville, Long Island and Sergeant L. Martin, left taking notes.

Mary McLeod Bethune and USO Junior Hostesses at the Young Women's Christian Association during WWII, Washington, DC

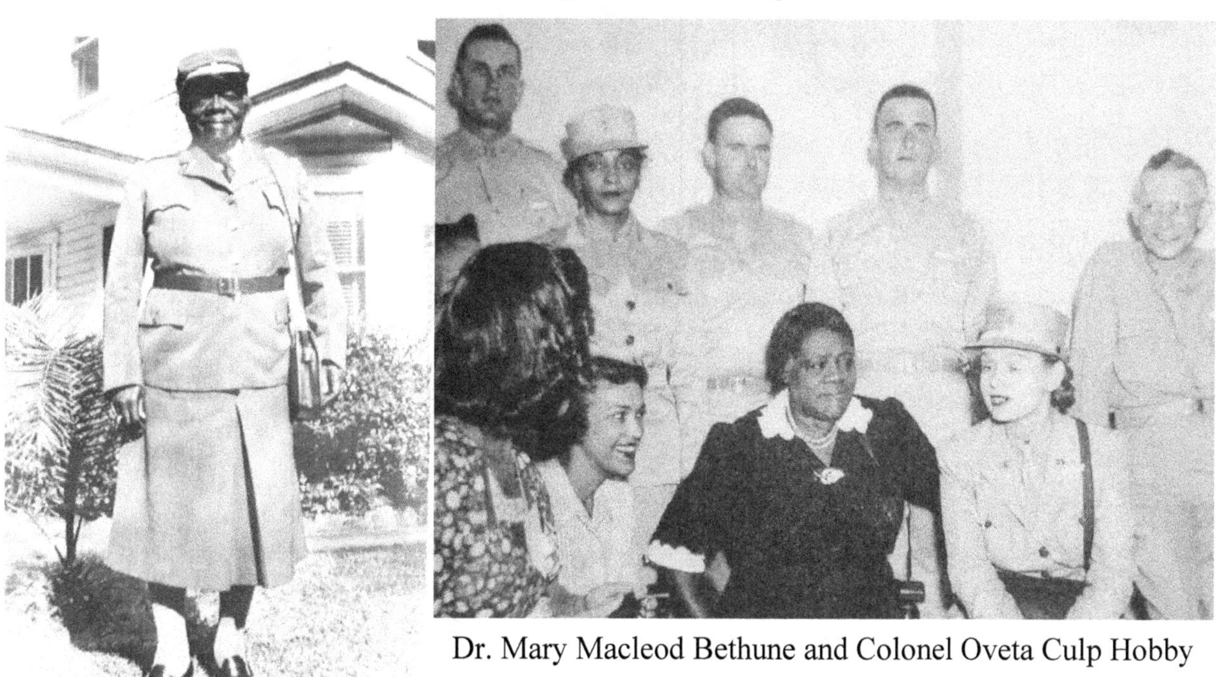

Dr. Mary Macleod Bethune and Colonel Oveta Culp Hobby

Women!
Answer
America's
Call

Mary McLeod Bethune talking with Vera Harrison of Wilberforce, Ohio and Mary Bordeaux of Louisville, Kentucky as new WAAC recruits began arriving at Des Moines, Iowa for training.

Charity Adams Early and Harriett West Waddy

Harriett West Waddy

Harriett West Waddy was born on June 20, 1904 in Jefferson City, Missouri. After high school graduation, she enrolled in Kansas State University. Waddy worked as Mary McLeod Bethune's aid after graduating from Kansas State University. Bethune was the director of the National Youth Administration's Division of Negro Affairs.

Harriett West Waddy was in the first WAAC Officer Candidate School at Fort Des Moines, Iowa in 1942. Waddy served as the WAC Director's advisor on Negro women and was the first Negro WAC promoted to the rank of major on August 23, 1943. She was promoted to Lieutenant Colonel in 1948. Colonel Waddy retired from the Armed Forces in 1952 and served in the Reserves until 1969.

Open Service Club for Negro WAACs

Surrounded by Negro WAAC auxiliaries, Colonel Don C. Faith, Commandant of the WAAC training camp at Fort Des Moines, is cutting the red, white, and blue ribbon formally opening the service club for Negro auxiliaries Saturday night. Captain J.G. Richardson, special service center is standing next to the Colonel. October 4, 1942

WAAC Comiskey Park

Marva Louis, wife of World Boxing Champion Joe Louis, leads drills at Comiskey Park, July 19, 1942

July 1942 Colonel Oveta Culp Hobby swears in first Negro female WAAC officer, Charity Early Adams

August/September 1942 WAAC Third Platoon, Company 1, Fort Des Moines standing in front of their commander, Captain Frank Stillman

WAAC Fort Des Moines, Iowa 1942

Women volunteering for the WAAC age requirements were 21-45 years of age, no dependents, at least 5 feet, and weighting a minimum of 100 pounds

First WAAC Officers Commissioned Fort Des Moines, Iowa 1942

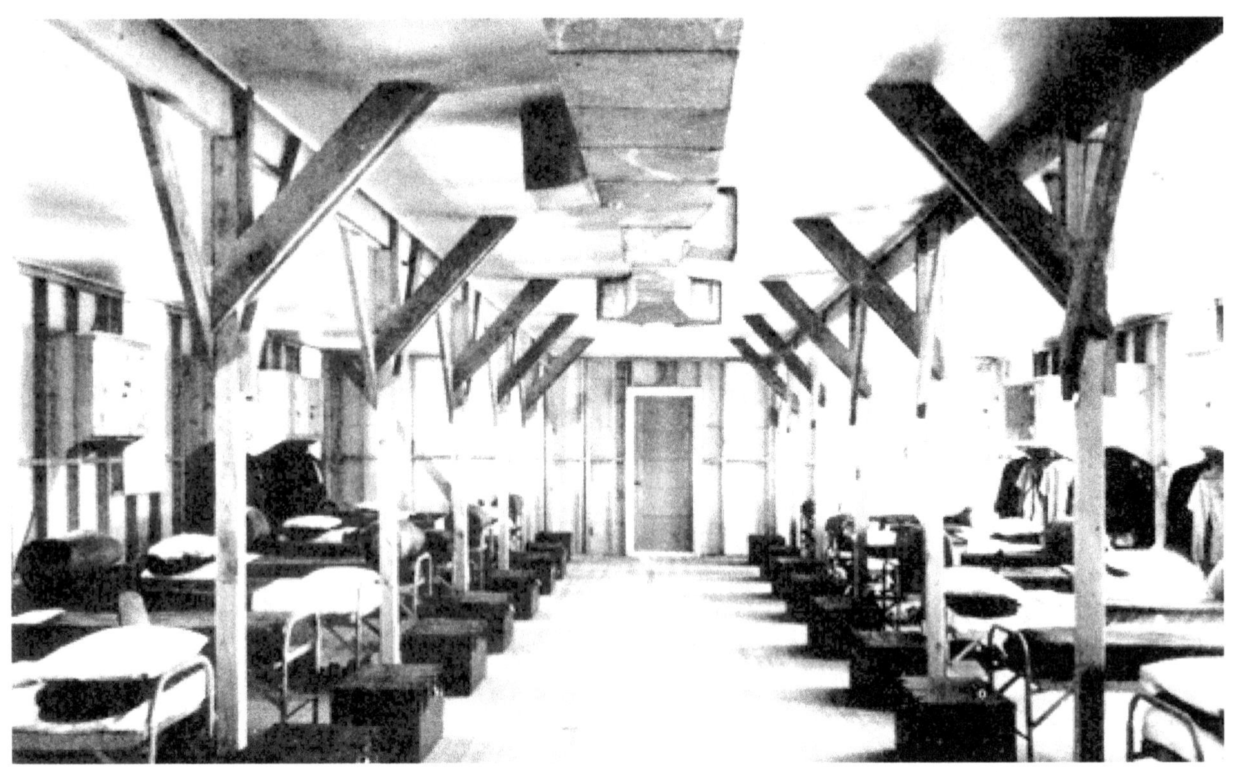

Des Moines WAC barracks

WACs relaxing in recreation room at Fort Des Moines, Iowa, 1942.

Military District of Washington

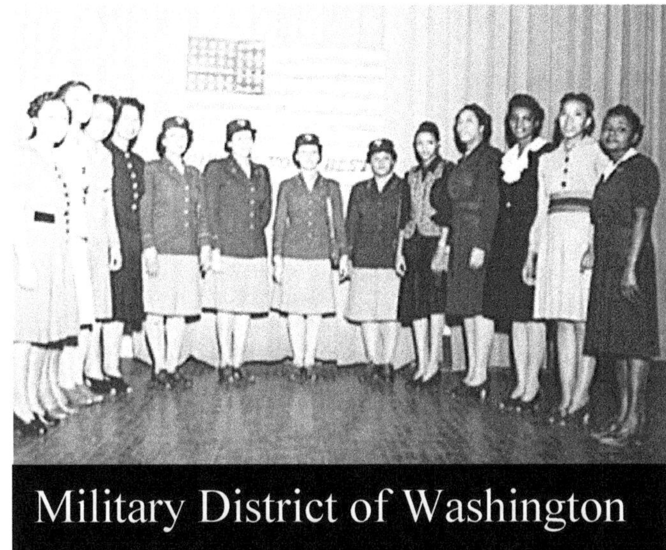

January 7, 1943 New WAAC recruits sworn in by Major Ina M. McFadden, recruiting officer Washington, DC at Cordoza High School. The recruits were part of a class of sixteen. Neppie Stoker Anderson, Joyce Pamela Arnold, Elizabeth Orlean Garrett, Juanita Green, Elise Givens, Farieta Hall, Lillie B. Harrison, Marie Humphrey, Nancy McCall, Evelyn F. Overton, Isabelle Peterson, Mittie Lee Thomas, Grace Elizabeth Thompson, Jeanne Cecelia Webster, Catherine Geneva Brown, and Ernestine Louise Woods. Major McFadden announced that the Military District of Washington was recruiting 150 Negro recruits.

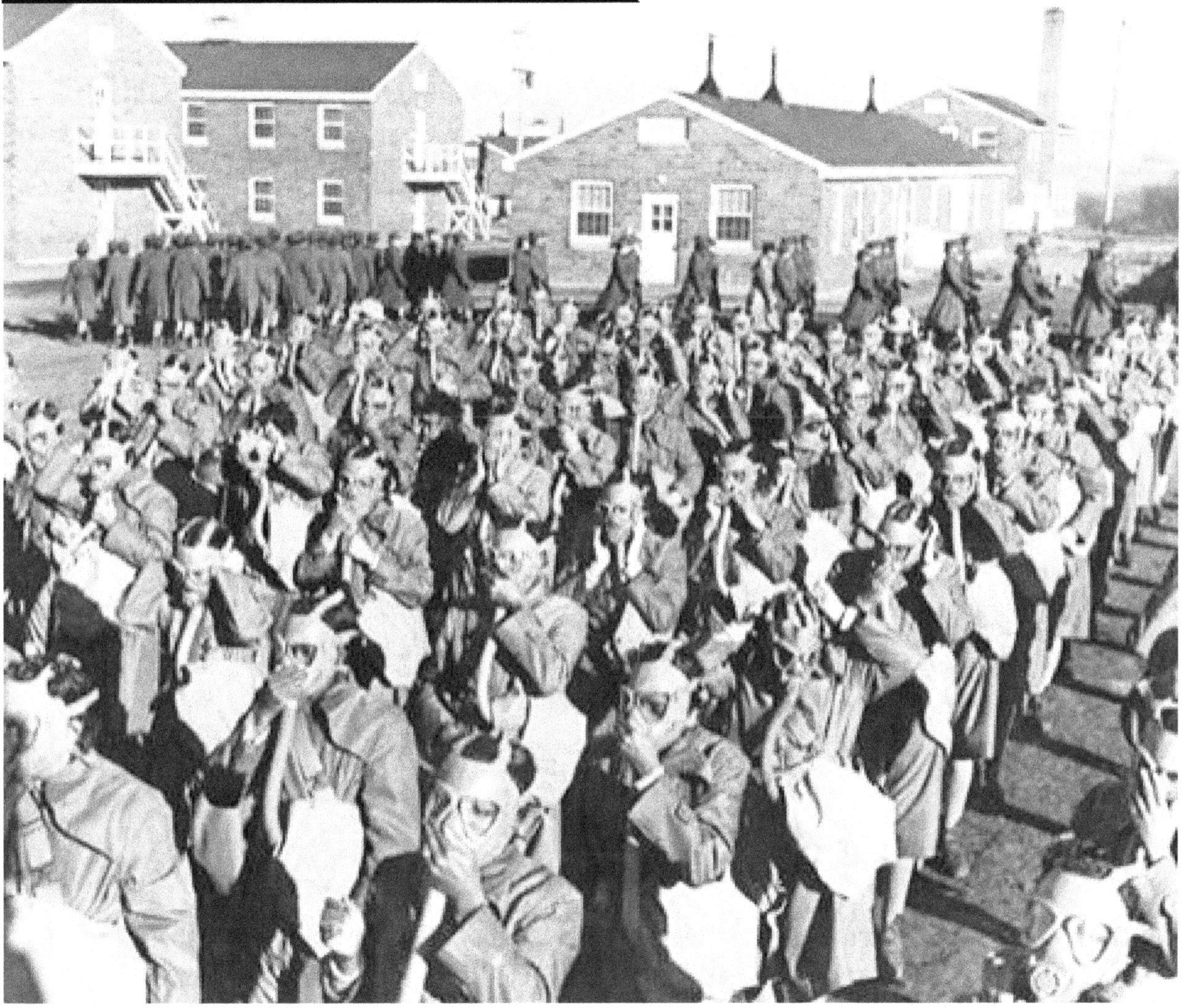

Members of the Women's Army Auxiliary Corps wearing gas masks and testing them for proper adjustment during a drill, First Women's Army Auxiliary Corps Training Center, 1943:

WAAC Captain Charity Adams drilling her company on the drill ground at the first WAAC Training Center, Fort Des Moines, Iowa (May 1943)

WAAC Auxiliaries, Florence Barbara Davis of Plaquemine, LA, Dorothy Lee Harris of Washington, Texas, Mildred Lucile Turk of Atlanta, Georgia, and Juanita Parisenne of Gainesville, Florida, in starched khaki uniforms being transported in the back of an Army deuce and a half truck to Fort Clark, Texas after completing their training at the WAAC First Training Center, Des Moines. 1943

TWINS NOW IN WAAC UNIFORM

Fort Des Moines, Iowa

First Negro Twins Hazel and Mazel Greer, 21 years old join the Women's Army Auxiliary Corps, Fort Des Moines, Iowa

Negro WACs Celebrate Birthday of USO Center

Keo Way USO Club, 1333 Keosauqua Way, observed its first anniversary along with 200 Negro WACs, servicemen, and volunteer host and hostesses celebrated the occasion in Mardi Gras style. They danced and sang, watched several acts, and birthday cake. These WACs enjoyed the fun while they could before reporting back to Fort Des Monies at 11pm, February 27, 1942.

WAAC candidate in gas mask, 1942

Vera G. Campbell

Vera G. Campbell member of the first class of officer candidates in the WAAC, 1942

Third Platoon, First Company, WAAC First Training Center
Negro Officers

Charity E. Adams
Myrtle E. Anderson
Verneal M. Austin
Geraldine G. Bright
Abbie N. Campbell
Mildred E. Carter
Cleo V. Daniels
Sarah E. Emmert
Ruth L. Freeman
Elizabeth C. Hampton
Bessie M. Jarrett
Alice M. Jones
May L. Lewis
Veolis H. Lynch
Charline J. May
Glendora Moore
Doris M. Norrel
Gertrude J. Peebles
Jessie L. Ward
Harriett B. White

Francis Alexander
Violet W. Askins
Mary A. Bordeaux
Annie L. Brown
Vera G. Campbell
Thelma J. Cayton
Natalie F. Donaldson
Geneva V. Ferguson
Evelyn F. Greene
Vera A. Harrison
Dovey M. Johnson
Mary F. Kearney
Ruth A. Lucas
Ina M. Mac Fadden
Mary L. Miller
Sarah Murphy
Mildred L. Osby
Corrie S. Sherard
Harriet M. West

Charity E. Adams

Dovey M. Johnson

Prairie View A&M Graduates Annie Lois Brown Wright, Ruth L. Freeman, Geraldine Bright, and Alice Marie Jones volunteered for the first WAAC Officer Candidate Class at Des Moines, Iowa.

Ruth Alice Lucas was the first Negro promoted to Colonel in the United States Air Force. After graduating from Tuskegee Institute in 1938, she joined the Women's Army Auxiliary in 1942. Colonel Lucas was one of the first Negro women to attend the Joint Forces Staff College located in Norfolk, Virginia. She transferred from the Army to the Air Force in 1947.

Dr. Allie Geraldine Harshaw

Dr. Allie Geraldine Harshaw was the first African American female Air Force Master Sergeant to retire with 30 years of service. She graduated from Tuskegee Institute in 1940. Harshaw enlisted in the WAAC on April 2, 1943 and retired from the Air Force on November 30, 1973 after serving in World War II, Koren War, and Vietnam.

During World War II, Harshaw was a physical therapy technician serving Tuskegee Airmen near Columbus, Ohio. Throughout her military career, she received training as an X-ray technician and completed her PHD in Human Behavior from the International University of San Diego, California.

On March 29, 2007, Harshaw was awarded the Congressional Gold Medal from President Bush.

WAAC, WAC, and WAF Duty Stations

Fort Des Moines, Iowa
Fort Dix, New Jersey
Atlantic City, New Jersey
Lockborne, Ohio
Cheyenne, Wyoming
Chanute Air Force Base, Illinosis
Sealand Air Force Base,
Wales London, England
March Air Force Base, California
Vandenberg Air Force Base, California

Henry Draws the WACs

As did Sergeant Joe Louis in his recent refereeing stint in Des Moines, Henry Armstrong, former holder of three world ring crowns, drew a host of Negro WAC admirers in a visit to the Fort Des Monies army post. Armstrong makes another bid on his comeback trail here at the Coliseum tonight against Jackie Byrd, Blytheville, Arkansas, puncher, February 29, 1942.

DES MONIES, IOWA

Honor Negro WAACs, July 25, 1942
A WAAC to Address Negro Club Women, September 18, 1942

Director for Negro Center, October 6, 1942

Negro WAAC to Preach, November 14, 1942

Negro WAAC Officers in Recruiting Talk Here Wednesday, December 12, 1942

Negro Recruits Sought by WAAC, December 13, 1942

Negro WAAC Recruiter Here, December 14, 1942

Negro WAAC Officers in Recruiting Talk Here Wednesday, December 17, 1942

Negro Officer Seeks Recruits for WAAC, December 16, 1942

Lt. Mays Tells WAAC Program in Tour of State, December 24, 1942

Discrimination Against WAACs is Charged, January 11, 1943

Church to Hear WAAC Officer, February 20, 1943

373 New Negro WAACs Coming, March 1, 1943

A Son Born to a WAAC, April 30, 1943

New Group of WAACs Assigned Cooks, Bakers, and Administration, May 13, 1943

WAAC Dies After Crash, May 17, 1943

New Chaplain for WAACs, May 17, 1943

Ministers Protest Discrimination of WAACs at Park, May 27, 1943

Five More WACs Get Commission, July 15, 1943

Negro WAACs Entertained at Tea

The Negro Community Center held a tea for 40 Negro members of the Women's Army Auxiliary Corps on Sunday for the women stationed at Fort Des Moines. Getting acquainted are (left to right) Mrs. Vera Spangler, 1172 Fourteenth Street, a member of the center's committee: Mrs. Jessie Ward of New York, New York; Mrs. Marjorie Mason, WAAC hostess; and Miss Verneal Austin of New York, New York, July 27, 1942.

Negro WAACs and Soldiers Entertained

It was home-cooked food for Negro soldiers and Negro WAACs Saturday night at the Blue Triangle Branch of the YWCA, 1407 Center Street. At a table are Miss Noel Campbell, 23, an officer candidate, of Tuskegee, Alabama; Mrs. Helen Beshears, 1127 Eleventh Street, Chairman of the Blue Triangle YWCA Branch Committee of Management; and Private Robert Parker, 22, Des Moines, August 9, 1942.

USO Center for Negro WAACs and Soldiers

WAACs, Alma Huff Berry of Houston, Texas, Consuelo Blank of Keokuk, Louisiana, and Nancie E. Ellison of Indianapolis, Indiana, relaxing at the temporary United Service Organizations Center, at 1201 Keosauqua Way, for Negro soldiers and members of the WAAC auxiliaries. October 23, 1942

Negro Service Men Entertained at WAAC Center

A group of Negro Officer Candidates attending the army school at Grinnell College were guests at the Negro WAAC USO Center, Twelfth Street and Keosauqua Way. Here they listen to juke box records with two Negro WAACs in training at Fort Des Moines, November 8, 1942.

All Negro WAC Band Plays at Grinnell

The band all colored ladies from Fort Des Moines make excellent music and play with skill and enthusiasm. They are clever at marching and the many who heard them at the concert were very pleased. The girls started out with little or no help from anyone and soon developed into a real playing and marching band, June 29, 1944

Jennie Dee Moton

Base Librarian PFC Jennie Dee Moton daughter of Jennie Booth and Dr. Robert Russa Moten, second president of Tuskegee Institute, was born in Tuskegee, Alabama. She was the youngest of five children. She attended school in Tuskegee and after graduating from Hampton Institute with bachelor degree in English and French, Moton joined the army. Moton completed basic trainig at Fort Des Monies, Iowa. Her first duty assignment was at Walla Walls, Washington. Moten was later assigned to Wendover, Utah before being stationed at Sioux City as the base librarian. Moten was eventually assigned to 6888th to the Special Service Office as an entertainment specialist and a member of the WAC-Acts who performed for the British troops.. She attained the rank of sergenant before being discharged.

Negro WAC Pastor Named

First Lieutenant King D. Reddick appointed chaplain for the Negro WACs at Fort Des Moines headquarters, July 9, 1943.

DES MONIES, IOWA

Ministers Protest Discrimination of WAACs at Park, May 27, 1943

Five More WACs Get Commission, July 15, 1943

Negro WAC Major, September 23, 1943

Open Exhibit of Negro Art, November 7, 1943

Award to Negro WAC Musician, November 20, 1943

Negro WAC Unit to Sioux City Air Base, April 2, 1944

Negro WACs at Air Base Perform Important Jobs, April 23, 1944

Pella's Tulip Fete Draws 4,000 People, May 19, 1944

Marching Down the Field, June 19, 1944

Negro WAC Band Play Here Saturday Eve, June 19, 1944

WAC Negro Band Gives Fine Concert, June 26, 1944

Negro WAC Band is Discontinued, July 21, 1944

WAVES to Enroll Negroes Next Year, October 29, 1944

First Negro Woman Joins the WAVES, November 14, 1944

Nurse Draft Not Needed Group Told February 10, 1945

The Wacs . . . what they are

WAC stands for Women's Army Corps. When you join the WAC you are in the Army of the United States. You don't pull triggers or fire cannon on the battlefront, but you take over a vital Army job behind the lines — a job that is essential to our victory.

The WAC is organized exactly like any other corps of our Army. Pay and allowances are the same as for Army men. A Wac wears a uniform as smart as any soldier's — and she's as proud of it as he is.

Being a Wac is one of the important jobs a woman can do in this war. It's serious work. It's the challenge of a lifetime to any American woman.

President Franklin D. Roosevelt recently said: "Those of us who have seen and know the work the Wacs are doing, throughout the military establishments of our country and in foreign stations, have only admiration and respect for the spirit, the dignity, and the courage they have shown."

1st Company 3rd Regiment First WAAC Training Center, Fort Des Moines, Iowa May 8, 1943
Lieutenant E. Berryhill, Commanding; Lieutenant S. Lassman, Executive Officer; Lieutenant M. Hilliard, Recreation Officer; Lieutenant V. Freeman, Supply Officer;

Mary McLeod Bethune and Eleanor Roosevelt visiting Lucy D. Slowe Hall, women's dormitory for Negro war workers Washington, DC, May 1943

Morning Register
Des Moines, Iowa

Major Charity Adams was the second Negro WAC to be promoted to major. Post Commander Colonel Frank H. McCoskrie and Major Harriett M. West pin Adams gold oak leaves at Fort Des Moines, Iowa, 1943.

Negro WAC Becomes Major

Maj. Charity E. Adams (center) Tuesday received gold oak leaves and congratulations at Fort Des Moines on her promotion from Col. Frank H. McCoskrie, post commandant, and Maj. Harriet M. West, Washington, D. C.

Capt. Charity E. Adams, Negro, supervisor of plans and training in headquarters of the first WAC training center at Fort Des Moines, Tuesday was promoted to the rank of major.

Major Adams is the second Negro member of the WAC to hold this rank. The other is Maj. Harriet M. West of Washington, D. C.

Major Adams is the daughter of the Rev. and Mrs. E. A. Adams of Columbia, S. C. The Rev. Dr. Adams is general secretary of the African Methodist Episcopal church there and supervises education in more than ten A.M.E. colleges in the country. He also is presiding elder and dean of theology at Allen university in Columbia.

Major Adams taught mathematics for four years at a high school at Columbia and was studying for her master's degree at Ohio State university when she joined the WAC.

She was graduated in the first Negro officer candidate class in August, 1942.

A graduate of Wilberforce university, Wilberforce, Ohio, Major Adams was selected for the 1937-38 edition of "Who's Who in American Universities and Colleges."

Her brother, Tech. Sergt. E. A. Adams, jr., is in the engineer corps of the army and is overseas.

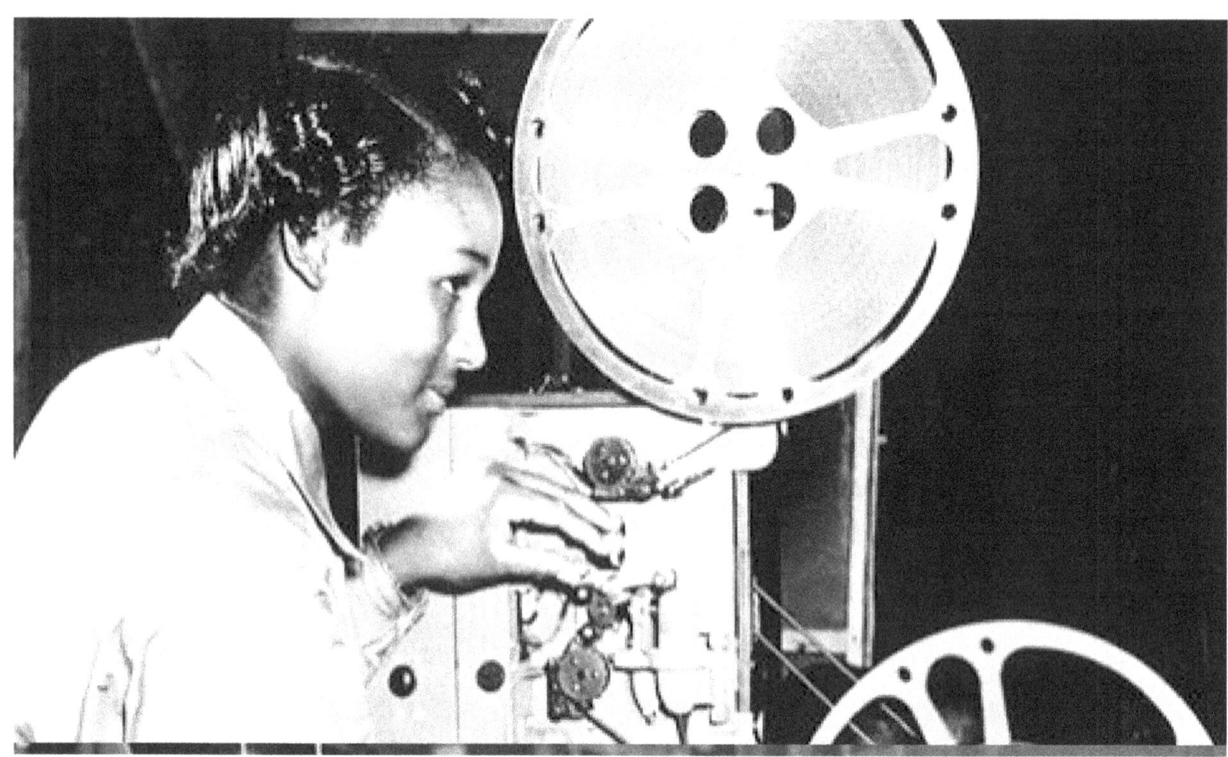

Tech 5 Susan Baptist, Whitehaven, Tennessee, projectionist showing training films and motion pictures to soldiers to help train and build morale at Fox Hills.

WACs identifying incorrectly addressed mail for soldiers Camp Brekinridge, Kentucky, November 30, 1943.

Captain Lois Freeman swearing in a group of Negro girls, Rosalia Bennett, Mae Harper, Eunice Williams, Lois Oauline, and Doris Murphy, at the Colored Service Member Center in Chicago, Illinois on March 11, 1944. Heavy Weight Boxing Champion Joe Lois was on hand to welcome them to the Army.

WAC Officer Candidate Class ND. 50 graduates May 20, 1944 Third WAC Training Center, Fort Oglethorpe, Georgia

First WAC Training Center Fort Des Moines, Iowa July 24, 1944

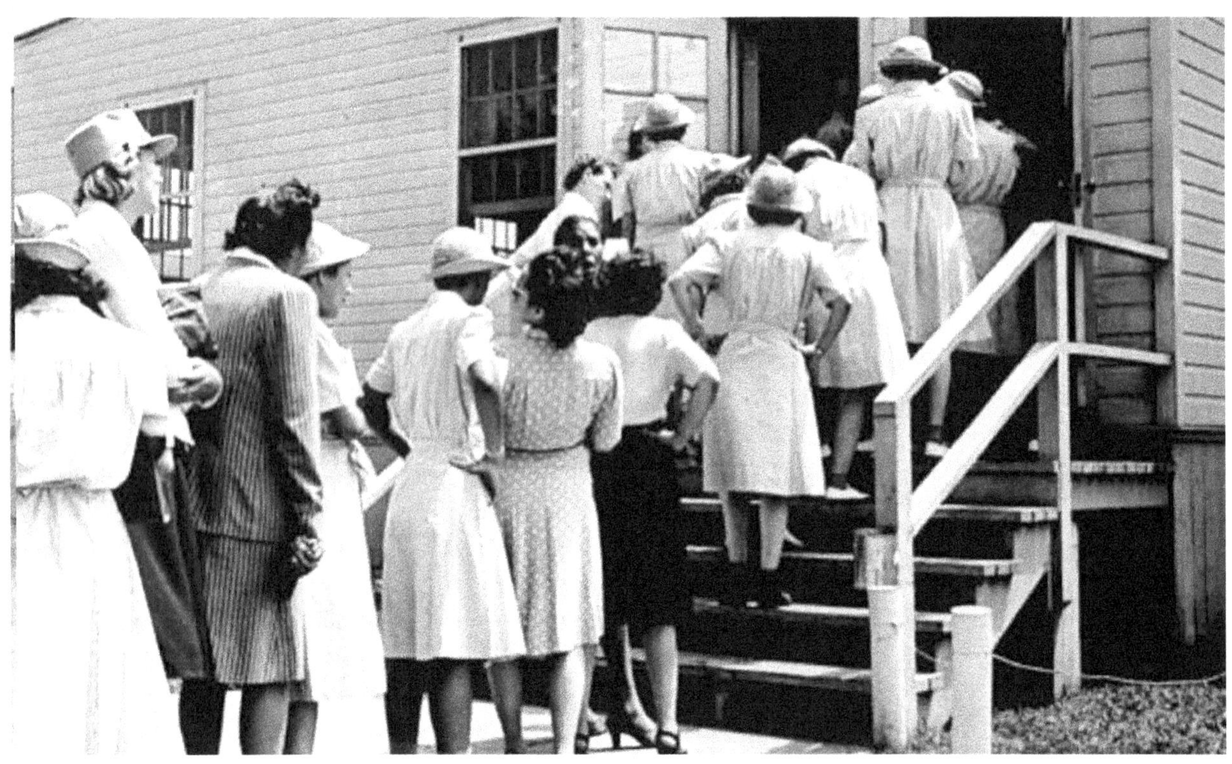

WACs entering the mess hall

Company 6, 3rd Regiment First WAC Training Center Fort Des Moines, Iowa August 8, 1944
Lieutenant Vera G. Campbell Commanding Officer, Lieutenant Thelma B. Brown Second in Command, Lieutenant Julia H. Williams Supply Officer, Lieutenant Helma D. Williams Recreational Officer

Company 6, 3rd Regiment First WAC Training Center Fort Des Moines, Iowa August 15, 1945
Lieutenant Vera G. Campbell Commanding Officer, Lieutenant Verdia M. Hickambotton Second in Command, Lieutenant Margaret A. Curtis Supply Officer

Lieutenants Roby Gill, Beaumont, Texas; and Leola M. Green, Houston, Texas; sitting at a table and working on a jigsaw puzzle while Lieutenants Mattie L. Aikens, Macon, Georgia; Zola Mac Lang, Chicago, Illinois; and Ellen L. Robinson, Hackensack, New Jersey assist and look on. These were US Army Nurses sent to Liberia.

WACs learning to type, 1945

Nealie Zenora Hoskins

Nealie Zenora Hoskins one of twelve children was born on August 17, 1917 in Fostoria, Montgomery County, Texas to Leader Cotton and Elder William Hoskins. She joined the Church of the Living God and was baptized by her father Elder William Hoskins. Nealie attended grade school in Fostoria and moved to Beaumont, Texas to attend Charlton Pollard High School. The next year she moved to Waco, Texas and enrolled at Moore High and later Olive High. Nealie spent her last two years of high in Houston. Although she attended Jack Yates, Nealie graduated from Phillis Wheatley High School. After graduation, Nealie attended three years of college and worked as a hotel and restaurant manager before joining the WAACs.

Inspired by their grandfather's service during World War I, Nealie and her younger sister Leader enlisted in the Women's Auxiliary Army Corp officer training in for the duration of World War II or other emergencies, plus six months, subject to the discretion of the president or otherwise according to law. Because they were the first set of sisters to enlist, their picture was featured in newspapers around the world. The two were members of the first class of officers selected to attend officer training for the WAAC in August 1942.

The night they arrived at Fort Des Moines and marched to dinner, they were greeted by large signs bearing the word Colored regulating them to tables at the far end of the mess hall. One white woman from Georgia expressed that she did not want them in the same room. *I've never eaten with a Negro, and I'm not going to start now.* The women went through the line and got plates of food, but then Nealie (Boy), Leader (Shang), and several other Negro women overturned their plates on the table and marched out. They bought dinner at the Post Exchange and ate in their barracks. They had come expecting one corps; however, there was definitely two.

A day and a half later a white WAAC officer met with the women. Alerted of the problem, Dr. Bethune, First Lady Eleanor Roosevelt, and WAAC Colonel Oveta Culp Hobby came to Fort Des Moines to address the situation. Colonel Hobby told the white women that the Negro women had enlisted just like they had to perform the same job. Leader said *and we should be given the same kind of treatment.*

The Colored signs were removed from the mass hall, but the reality of segregation still remained. Dr. Bethune explained to the Negro WAACs that segregation was a reality and they had to live with it. She stressed how important they were to the race. *We are making history here today. The Negro women whose faces are turned this way are depending upon you to represent us on the ground floor of this dramatic new program. Out if millions of us, you have been selected... for a grave responsibility-a challenging responsibility.*

The Negro WAACs were inspired by the call issued by Colonel Hobby *From now on you are soldiers, defending a free way of life…you wear the uniform of the Army of the United States. Respect the uniform. Respect all that it stands for.* At the end of training everyone hugged each other goodbye including the WAAC from Georgia.

After training at Fort Des Moines, Nealie was stationed at Fort Des Moines, Iowa, Fort Maxey near Paris, Texas, and Camp Stoneman, Pittsburg, California. Camp Stoneman was a large staging area for soldiers returning from the South Pacific. Nealie processed their discharge paperwork.

Nealie was discharged from the Army in 1946. She enrolled in Texas State University and received two undergraduate and two Masters degrees. Nealie and her sisters Leader and Blossie purchased land in Acres Homes. They opened and operated Hoskins' Grocery Store from May 1951 to 1976; Hoskins' Kindergarten September 1951 to 2006; and Hoskins' Historical Museum. They also spearheaded the construction of the Church of the Living God located at 911 Conklin Street. Nealie married Thomas Bowens, Jr. on August 7, 1954. In 1997, the Women's Memorial Wall was built in Arlington, Virginia as a dedication to all women that served in the military. Both Nealie and Leader names are engraved on the wall making their story forever a part of American History. Nealie loved history and travel. She traveled the world visiting historical sites.

Nealie was affectionally known as *Aunt Boy*. She dedicated her life to influencing and inspiring young people to *dream big to overcome obstacles.*

Leader Ledora Hoskins Jackson born on July 19, 1919 died July 3, 2015 one year of college December 29, 1942/

Plate officer semi dress uniform
1945 Pinks and Greens Uniform was a dark olive drab elastique wool material for the jacket and light drab wool skirt

Fort Huachuca

The 32nd and 33rd Women's Auxiliary Army Companies at Fort Huachuca were the first all Negro contingent of WAACs assigned to a military installation in the United States. Before reporting to Fort Huachuca on December 4, 1942, the 200 auxiliaries trained for six weeks at Fort Des Moines. Fort Huachuca was the largest Negro army post in the country under the leadership of Negro commissioned officers, Irma Jackson Cayton, Vera Ann Harrison, Frances Alexander, Violet Askins, Natalie Donaldson, Mary Kearney, and Corrie Sherard. The WAACs performed clerical and administrative work as stenographers, typists, telephone switchboard, operators, clerks, messengers, receptionists, and motor pool drivers and mechanics.

Enlisted personnel barracks

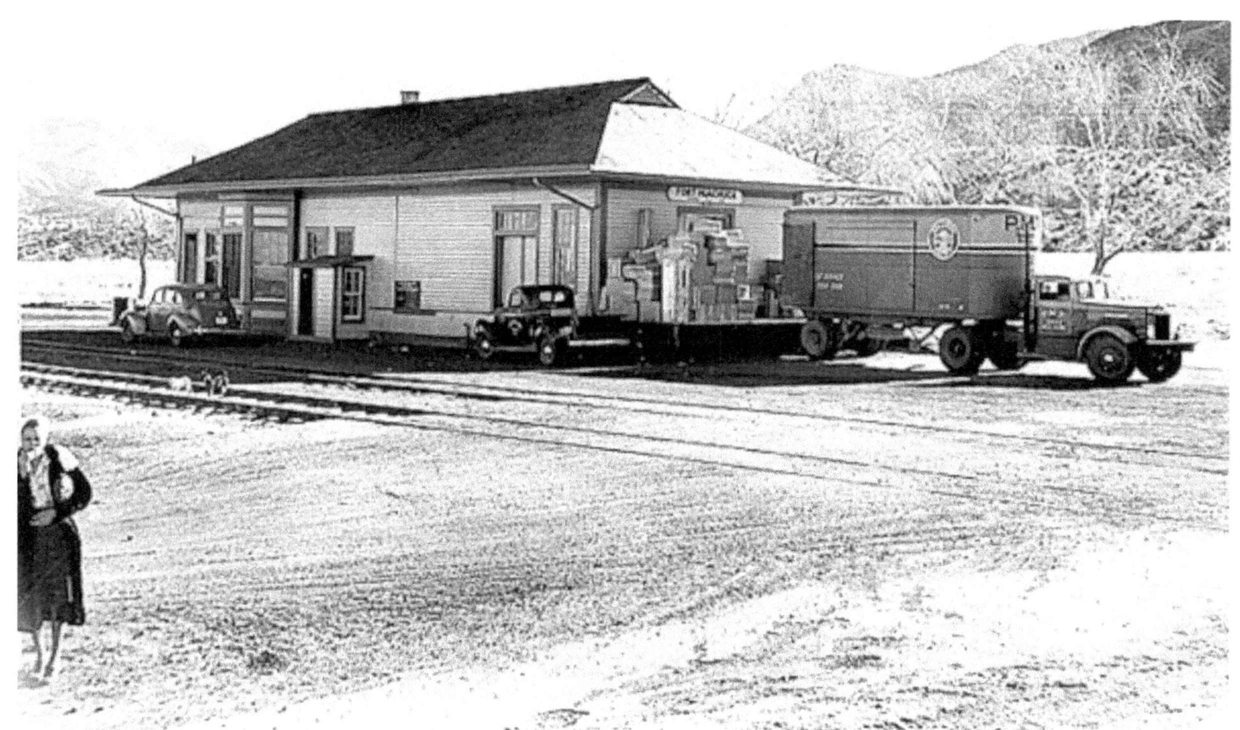

Southern Pacific Railroad Station Fort Huachuca, 1943

Fort Huachuca Headquarters

JANUARY 17, 1943

THE LARGEST NEGRO MILITARY COMMAND IN THE WORLD

DOUGLAS, DAILY DISPATCH.

DECEMBER 5, 1942

2 Companies of Smartly Dressed WAACs Arrive at Ft. Huachuca To Begin Serving With Army

FORT HUACHUCA, Dec. 4 (AP)—The 32nd and 33rd Post Headquarters Company, Women's Army Auxiliary Corps—the first to be assigned to an army post in this country—arrived here today on a special train from Fort Des Moines, Iowa.

The WAAC pulled into a railroad siding with approximately [illegible] unofficial welcomers greeting them. Five pullman cars, one kitchen and one baggage car comprised the WAAC railway entourage.

Third officers who accompanied the WAAC to this post on the train were Frances C. Alexander, Toledo, Ohio, who served as commander of the 32nd Company; Violet Askins, Chicago, Ill., and officers from the 33rd Company who arrived today included third officers Natalie F. Donaldson, New York City; Corrie Sherard, Atlanta, Ga., and Mildred L. Osby, Washington, D. C., war department bureau of public relations officer.

WAAC officers who welcomed the arrivals were third officers Hazel F. [illegible], director of the Women's Army Auxiliary Corps in the ninth service command, with headquarters at Fort Douglas, Utah; Harriet M. West, of WAAC headquarters, Washington, D. C.; Vera Anne Harrison, Wilberforce, Ohio; and Irma J. Cayton, Chicago.

Army officers who accompanied the WAACS on the train were Captain Nathan Cohen, surgeon; First Lieut. Harry Crowley, train commander, both of whom will return to Fort Des Moines immediately.

Col. Edwin N. Hardy, post commander, welcomed the WAAC. The 368th Infantry band was present, as were a platoon of 36 men from the post's service command military police battalion and a platoon of 36 men from the ordnance detachment here.

The WAAC left the train in military formation, and headed by the band and accompanied by the two platoons, marched to their barracks, where they were properly dressed in formation.

Col. Hardy, flanked by officers of his staff and several WAAC officers [illegible] delivered an address of welcome and instruction in which he stressed "you represent the venture of our government in putting the women of America into uniform as a part of our armed forces."

Col. Hardy declared that he had the greatest confidence in the high standards that the WAAC will set at this post for the Women's Army Auxiliary Corps.

Colonel Hardy with two WAAC officers taking retreat formation.

First members of the 32nd and 33rd Women's Army Auxiliary Corps to arrive at Fort Huachuca on December 4, 1942 are detrained. They are welcomed by members of the 93d Infantry Division.

The 32nd Women's Army Auxiliary Corps Company arrived at Fort Huachuca on December 4, 1942. Lieutenant Cayton Company Commander, seated in the center. Hazel M. Russell 10th from right, 2nd row, served at Fort Huachuca from 1961-62 as Sergeant First Class, WAC.

WAAC cooks prepare dinner for the first time in new kitchen at Fort Huachuca, Arizona on December 5, 1942

32nd and 33rd WAAC Companies enjoying a meal in the mess hall at Camp Huachuca, December 9, 1942

WAAC Officers Vera Harrison and Irma J. Cayton shopping for lamps and other accessories for the recreation hall soon after their arrival at Fort Huachuca, Arizona in 1942.

Parading on the Old Post.

32nd WAACs Company marching to their barracks, 1942

WAACs arrive at Fort Huachuca, Arizona December 1942

WAAC January 1, 1943

32nd Company standing at attention during training at Fort Huachuca, Arizona

On December 8, 1942, Auxiliaries Ruth Wade and Lucille Mayo demonstrate their ability to service trucks as taught them during the processing period at Fort Des Moines and put into practice at Huachuca, Arizona.

Members of WAAC in the motor pool at Fort Huachuca, Arizona, 1943

WAC making emergency repairs, Fort Huachuca

WAC Army Truck Driver Priscilla Taylor 1943

WAACs trained in the handling of all types of trucks await the command start their vehicles at the post motor pool, Fort Huachuca, Arizona, December 1942

Elizabeth Tex Williams

Elizabeth Tex Williams was born in 1924. She became her career in Houston, Texas as an assistant with Stanley Reddick Art Studio. Williams completed basic training at Fort Des Moines, Iowa. After basic training, Williams was sent to Fort Huachuca, Arizona as a photo lab assistant. There she photographed air maneuvers and defense intelligence. Williams was the first woman and first Negro to graduate from the Photo Division in Fort Monmouth, New Jersey. She became the WAC's official army photographer documenting Negro military women and their contributions to the war efforts.

Members of the 32nd and 33rd Companies' Women's Army Auxiliary Corps basketball team take some time to relax from their duties with a game of basketball at Fort Huachuca, Arizona

Triple Wedding on June 5, 1943 Chaplin James A. Wactor marrying Mattie Elliott, Irene Stewart, and Etta Mae Pullman respectfully Captain Willie D. Thompson, Private First Class Allen A. Harris and Private Erlie Gales

Triple Wedding Breakfast in the mess hall for the MP Detachment, Fort Huachuca, Arizona June 5, 1943

93d BLUE HELMET

Fort Huachuca, Arizona · 93d BLUE HELMET FRIDAY, SEPT. 18, 1942 · Volume I, No. 1

Victory Show Great Success Here

"Cabin In The Sky" Cast Entertains Soldier Audience

By JACK PALMS

Before the largest audience ever assembled in the 93d Division Open-Air Arena, the Hollywood Victory Committee, headed by Clarence Muse, gave a variety show that was received with roars of applause from the beginning to the end, Sunday afternoon and night, Sept. 6.

Coming directly from Hollywood, where the members of the show are appearing in the MGM production of "Cabin in the Sky," these performers staged a show, the equal of which Fort Huachuca has never seen.

The audience put its stamp of approval on Hattie Morrison's "boogie-woogie" piano, calling for more.

Chinkie Grimes was called again and again for encores of her red-hot dancing and singing. Sunshine Sammy, teaming with Effert "Noody" Bowman, started applause that grew in volume when Princess Luana and Woodie Strode came on stage, Princess Luana doing hula-hula and singing Hawaiian songs with Woodie singing also.

Olive Ball sang "Ol' Black Joe" in bass, then in soprano she sang "Homing" then climaxed her appearance on the stand with her very comical "Instructions In Public Speaking."

Lena Horne sang "I Got A Gal In Kalamazoo," "You Are My Thrill," and others, as only Lena can sing them. Pepper Neely, Alford Moore and two enlisted men made this a well-rounded show. The two enlisted men were, Rico Harrison and Corp Effert "Noody" Bowman. Rico sang "This Love of Mine" and "Noody" teamed with Sunshine Sammy.

Leana Horne with the baseball team of the 1922 Service Command Unit, 1943

Joe Louis shaking Colonel Edwin Hardy's hand

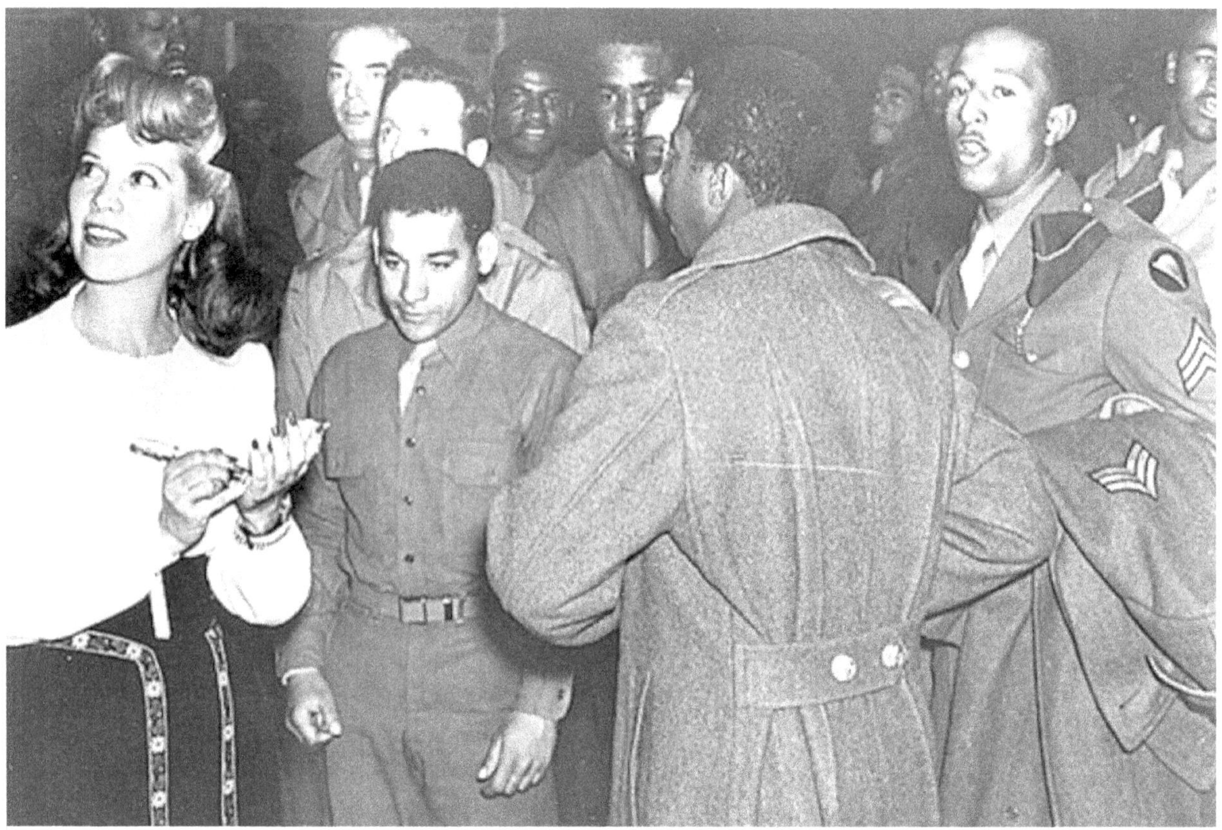

Dinah Shore signing autographs for members of the 93rd Division at Fort Huachuca, 1943

Brigadier General F.W. Moorman inspects the WAC Detachment, Fort Huachuca July

Lew Davis at art show of Negro artist at the Officers' Mountainview Club at Huachuca, 1943

The 404th Army Services Forces Band formed at Fort Des Moines, Iowa in 1943

Staff Sergeant Leonora Hull Brown, Director
404th WAC Band

Staff Sergeant Leonora Hull Brown, Director
404th WAC Band
Savoy Ballroom, Chicago, Illinois
May 24, 1945

WACs pass in review on the Lower Parade Field, Fort Huachuca, 1943

Colonel Hardy with members of the WAAC contingent on the Upper Parade Field, Fort Huachuca

Funeral possession for Sergeant Andrew J. Duke Wells, Fort Huachuca, September 1943

CAMP
ATTERBURY
1942

Group of Camp Atterbury WAACs relaxing after a long day of work, playing with a small dog June 22, 1943

Camp Atterbury

Camp Atterbury located on 40,000 acres 30 miles from Indianapolis, Indiana was named after General W.W. Atterbury. General W.W. Atterbury was the Director of Transportation of the AEF during World War I and President of the Pennsylvania Railroad System. The first officers arrive at Camp Atterbury in June 1942 and the first largest scale movement of military personnel in July.

Servicemen of the 751st Medical Sanitary Company and servicewomen of the Medical Section, 3561st Service Unit, Women's Army Corps dancing at Service Club No. 3 at Camp Atterbury, Indiana.

Members of the Columbus Rotary Club presenting books to officers working at Service Club No. 1 at Camp Atterbury, Indiana.

First Sergeant and Noncommissioned Officers

The eight members of the enlisted administrative force of the Medical Section, 3561st Service Unit of the Women's Army Auxiliary Corps (WAAC) following a regular morning conference at Camp Atterbury, Indiana. (No. 113 F) Seated in front (left to right): Auxiliary Dorothy L. Howard, 1st Sergeant Thelma Lytle, and Aux. Gladys G. Jones. Standing behind (front left to right): Auxiliaries Gertrude Slaughter, Irene C. Figgins, Catherine G. Brown, Eulah M. Bailey, and Supply Sergeant Laverne Grose. July 9, 1943

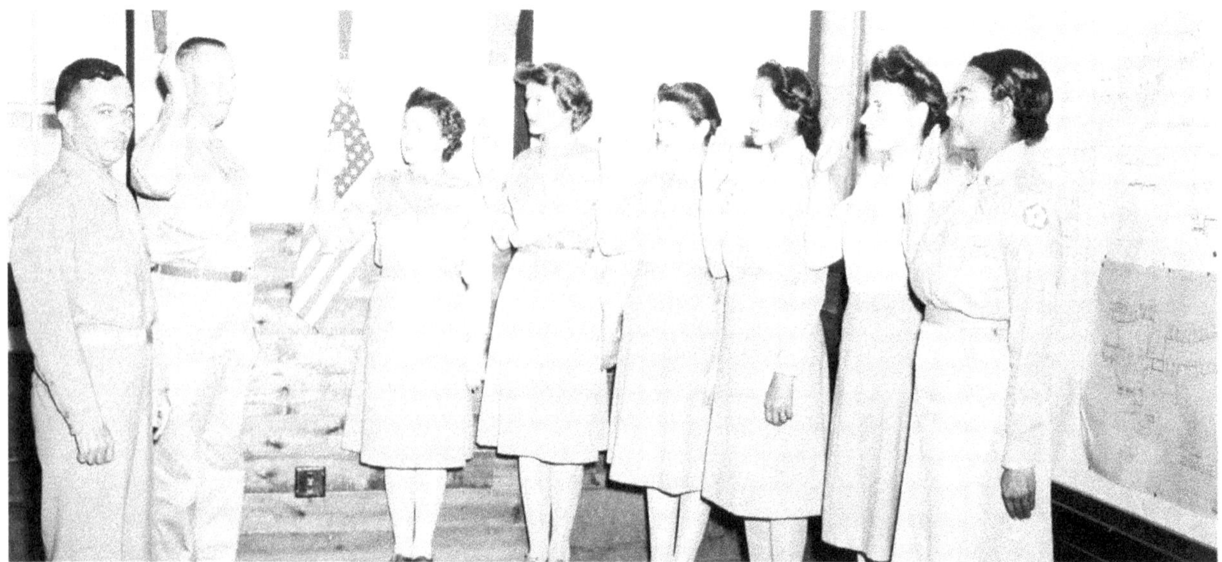

Post Adjutant Captain E.D. Keith with Post Commander, Colonel Welton M. Modisette, swearing in six WAAC officers, Captain Elizabeth A. Wilbern, Lieutenants Mary L. Porter, Mildred Peterson, Sarah E. Murphy, Jeanne G. Childs, and Camille F. Thomas, at Camp Atterbury, Indiana. September 3, 1943

Post Commander Colonel Welton M. Modisette award five officers of the 3561st Service Unit WAC Service Ribbons, September 24, 1943.

Two officers presenting WAC Service Ribbons to enlisted members of the Headquarters Section of the 3561st Service Unit, September 24, 1943.

Members of the Medical Section 3561st Service Unit at their formal oath taking ceremony admitting them into the Women's Army Corps at Camp Atterbury, Indiana. These women were prior members of the WAAC.

Graduating class of WACs celebrating their induction into the United States Army, August 10, 1943

References

1. 2 Units Sent to Huachuca (1942, December 12), *Houston Informer.*
2. 373 New Negro WAACs Coming (1943, March 1), *Register Des Moines, Iowa.*
3. A Son Born To A WAAC (1943, April 30), *Evening Tribune Des Moines, Iowa.*
4. All Negro WAC Band Plays At Grinnell (1944, June 29), *Herald Register Grinnell, Iowa.*
5. Award to Negro WAC Musician (1943, November 20), *Morning Register Des Moines, Iowa.*
6. Based Librarian (1944, October 22), *Journal Sioux City, Iowa.*
7. Brenham, Texas Girl Is One of Two WAAC Mess Officers (1942, December 12), *Houston Informer.*
8. Buffalo Soldiers National Museum, Houston, Texas.
9. Campbell, Darwin. (2016, November 6). Meet Burnadine Bunny Fraser 95 Year Old WW II Veteran. African American News & Issues. Retrieved from http://www.afrmnews.com/meet-burnadine-bunny-fraser-95-year-old-wwii-veteran/.
10. Church To Hear WAAC Officer (1943, February 20), *Evening Tribune Des Moines, Iowa.*
11. Click, Negro WAAC joins Army to help her country and race November 1942 p.19
12. Director for Negro Center (1942, October 6), *Register Des Moines, Iowa.*
13. Discrimination Against WAACs Is Charged (1943, January 11), *Tribune Des Moines, Iowa.*
14. Draft Takes Farmer Early In February (1943, February 1), *Evening Tribune Des Moines, Iowa.*
15. Drake Heavy Choice Morning (1943, October 1), *Register Des Moines, Iowa.*
16. First All Black Combat Division Fort Huachuca, Arizona (1943), Life Magazine.
17. First Negro Woman Joins the WAVES (1944, November 14), *Morning Register Des Moines, Iowa.*
18. Five More WACs Get Commissions (1943, July 15), *Bystander Des Moines, Iowa.*
19. Fraser, Burnadine Unpublished Biography.
20. Henry Draws the WACs (1944, February 27), *Morning Register Des Moines, Iowa.*
21. Honor Negro WAACs (1942, July 25), *Tribune Des Moines, Iowa*
22. Hooper, Mildred Gates Unpublished Biography.
23. Hostess for Negro WAACs (1942, July 27), *Register Des Moines, Iowa.*
24. Houston Girl Is Choice (1942, December 12), *Houston Informer.*
25. Lt Mays Tells WAAC Program In Tour of State (1942, December 24), *Bystander Des Moines, Iowa.*
26. Marching Down The Field (1944, June 19), *Herald Register Grinnell, Iowa.*
27. Military Resources: Women In The Military https://www.archives.gov/files/research/african-americans/ww2-pictures/images/african-americans-wwii
28. Ministers Protest Discrimination of WAACs at Park (1943, May 27), *Bystander Des Moines, Iowa.*
29. Mullenbach, Cheryl Double Victory: How African American Women Broke Race and Gender Barriers
30. Negro Officer Seeks Recruits for WAAC (1942, December 10), *Gazette Cedar Rapids, Iowa.*
31. Negro Recruits Sought by WAAC (1942, December 13), *Courier Ottumwa, Iowa.*
32. Negro Service Men Entertained at WAAC Center (1942, November 8), *Register Des Moines, Iowa.*
33. Negro WAACs and Soldiers Entertained (1942, August 9), *Register Des Moines, Iowa*
34. Negro WAACs Entertained at Tea (1942, July 27), *Register Des Moines, Iowa.*

35. Negro WAAC Officer In Recruiting Talk Here Wednesday (1942, December 17), *Times Republican Marshalltown, Iowa.*
36. Negro WAAC Recruiter Here (1942, December 14), *Courier Ottumwa, Iowa.*
37. Negro WAAC Recruiting Officer to Be Here (1942, December 12), *Times Republican Marshalltown, Iowa.*
38. Negro WAAC To Preach (1942, November 14), *Tribune Des Moines, Iowa.*
39. Negro WAC A Major (1943, September 23), *News Newton, Iowa.*
40. Negro WAC Band In Concert Today (1945, April 26), *Morning Register Des Moines, Iowa.*
41. Negro WAC Band Is Discontinued (1944, July 21), *Morning Register Des Moines, Iowa.*
42. Negro WAC Band Will Play Here Saturday Eve (1944, June 19), *Herald Register Grinnell, Iowa.*
43. Negro WACs Celebrate Birthday of USO Center (1944, February 27), *Morning Register Des Moines, Iowa.*
44. Negro WAC Pastor Named (1943, July 9), *Evening Tribune Des Moines, Iowa.*
45. Negro WACs Perform Important Jobs (1944, April 23), *Journal Sioux City, Iowa.*
46. Negro WAC Unit to Sioux City Air Base (1944, April 2), 1944 *Morning Register Des Moines, Iowa.*
47. New Chaplin For WAAC (1943, May 17), *Tribune Des Moines, Iowa.*
48. New Group of WAACs Assigned Cooks-Bakers and Administration (1943, May 13), *Bystander Des Moines, Iowa.*
49. Nurse Draft Not Needed, Group Told (1945, February 10), *Morning Register Des Moines, Iowa.*
50. Nurses At Fort Des Moines Hospital (1944, April 2), *Bystander Des Moines, Iowa.*
51. Oldmagazinearticles.com
52. Open Exhibit of Negro Art (1943, November 7), *Morning Register Des Moines, Iowa.*
53. Open Service Club for Negro WAACs (1942, October 4), *Register Des Moines, Iowa*
54. Pella's Tulip Feta Draws 4,000 People (1944, May 19), *Morning Register Des Moines, Iowa.*
55. Receives Commission in Hospital (1943, January 21), *Register Des Moines, Iowa.*
56. Summernmotion.blogspot.com
57. Thorpe, Frances Wills Navy Blue and Other Colors
58. US Army Women's Museum
59. WAAC Dies After Crash (1943, May 17), *Tribune Des Moines, Iowa.*
60. WAAC's Invade, Take Big Fort Huachuca (1942, December 5), *Houston Informer.*
61. WAC Negro Band Gives Fine Concert (1944, June 26), *Herald Register Grinnell, Iowa.*
62. WAVES to Enroll Negroes Next Year (1944, October 24), *Morning Register Des Moines, Iowa.*
63. Womensmemorial.org

www.ingramcontent.com/pod-product-compliance
Lightning Source LLC
Chambersburg PA
CBHW050642150426
42813CB00054B/1154
9781953824066